SOCIAL
COMMERCE
UNLOCKED

Leveraging Social Media Platforms
to Boost E-Commerce Sales

Danielle Mead

CONTENTS

INTRODUCTION

Social commerce isn't just a trend – it's a fundamental shift in how people shop online. Over the past decade, social media has evolved from a place where users simply connect with friends and share updates to a powerful marketplace where brands and customers interact in real-time. Platforms like Instagram, Facebook, TikTok, and Pinterest have transformed into digital storefronts, allowing users to browse, engage, and even purchase products without ever leaving their favorite apps.

I've seen firsthand how businesses that embrace social commerce gain an edge over those that don't. Today's consumers expect convenience and seamless shopping experiences, and social platforms are delivering just that. The rise of mobile shopping, influencer marketing, and user-generated content has only accelerated this shift. If your store isn't leveraging social commerce, you're likely leaving money on the table.

Why Social Selling Is Crucial for E-Commerce Success

As an e-commerce store owner, you already know how important it is to drive traffic and convert visitors into customers. Social commerce helps bridge the gap between discovery and purchase, allowing you to meet customers where they are and reduce friction in the buying process.

One of the biggest advantages of social selling is the ability to create higher engagement and brand awareness. Social platforms give you the opportunity to interact directly with your audience through comments, direct messages, and live videos. By sharing engaging content such as short-form videos, interactive polls, and behind-the-scenes footage, you can keep your brand at the forefront of your customers' minds.

Another major benefit is the seamless shopping experience that social platforms provide. Features like Instagram Shopping and TikTok Shop allow users to browse products and check out without ever leaving the app. This removes unnecessary friction from the buying process, making it easier for customers to complete their purchase rather than abandoning their cart.

Social commerce also thrives on trust and social proof. Shoppers are more likely to trust recommendations from peers and influencers than traditional advertisements. That's why leveraging customer reviews, influencer partnerships, and user-generated content can be so powerful. The more credibility you build, the more likely customers will feel confident making a purchase from your store.

Finally, social platforms use powerful algorithms

to connect users with content they're most likely to engage with. This means that a well-optimized post showcasing your product has the potential to be seen by thousands – or even millions – of potential customers. I've found that businesses that actively engage with their audience and utilize social selling tools often see significant boosts in sales. The key is to treat your social media presence as an extension of your store rather than just a separate marketing channel. The more effort you put into building a community and fostering relationships, the more success you'll see.

Overview of Major Social Commerce Platforms

With so many social platforms available, it can be overwhelming to know where to start. Each one offers unique opportunities, and choosing the right one depends on your target audience and product type.

Instagram

Instagram has become a powerhouse for e-commerce, thanks to features like Instagram Shopping, product tags, and shoppable posts. If your store sells visually appealing products such as fashion, beauty, or home décor, Instagram is an essential platform. One of my go-to strategies is using Instagram Stories to showcase products in action and drive engagement through interactive polls and Q&A stickers. Additionally, Instagram Reels provide a fantastic way to showcase products in an entertaining and engaging format, while influencer collaborations can help expand your reach and credibility.

Facebook

Facebook remains a strong player in social commerce, particularly for brands targeting an older demographic. With Facebook Shops, you can create a fully integrated storefront, making it easy for users to browse and purchase products. Many brands have found success using Facebook Live to host product demonstrations and Q&A sessions, creating a direct and personal way to engage with customers. Messenger is another valuable tool for offering personalized recommendations and customer support. Running targeted Facebook Ads can also help you reach potential buyers based on their interests and behaviors, allowing you to scale your store's visibility.

TikTok

TikTok's explosive growth has made it a goldmine for brands that can create engaging, authentic content. The platform's short-form video format makes it easy to showcase products in an organic way. You can leverage TikTok's algorithm by jumping on trending challenges to increase visibility. TikTok Shop, combined with influencer marketing, makes it simple for users to discover and buy products directly within the app. Creating entertaining videos that highlight the value of your products is a great way to capture attention and drive sales.

Pinterest

Pinterest is ideal for businesses with highly visual products, especially in niches like home decor, DIY, fashion and cooking. Users on Pinterest are actively searching for inspiration and solutions, making them more likely to convert when they find the right product. Optimizing your Pins with strong keywords improves discoverability, while high-quality, vertical images make your products stand out. Linking Pins directly to your product pages ensures a smooth buying process, allowing interested users to make a purchase without extra steps.

***

Social commerce is more than just another sales channel – it's a way to build relationships, enhance customer experience, and drive long-term growth. Take a look at your current social media presence and ask yourself: Are you making it as easy as possible for customers to shop directly from your posts? If not, it's time to start harnessing the power of social commerce for your store.

But what if you're intimidated by social media or

scared to use it? In the next chapter, we'll discuss how to get over any concerns you might have about leveraging this powerful marketing channel.

OVERCOMING FEARS AND CONCERNS ABOUT USING SOCIAL MEDIA FOR YOUR BUSINESS

Over the years, I've spoken with many e-commerce store owners who hesitate to use social media for their business. The concerns vary – some don't like using social media personally, others worry about privacy, and many feel uncomfortable putting themselves "out there" for the world to see. If any of these fears resonate with you, you're not alone. The good news is that these concerns are understandable but can be overcome with the right mindset and strategies.

One of the most common worries I hear is, "I don't like social media and barely use it myself." If you're not an active social media user in your personal life, the idea of running an Instagram, Facebook, or TikTok account for your business can feel overwhelming or even unnecessary. But here's the reality – social media is where customers are discovering and engaging with brands. You don't need to love social media personally to leverage it effectively for your store. Think of it as a tool, just like email marketing or SEO, that helps you grow your business. You don't have to spend all day scrolling through social feeds. Just focus on using it strategically to connect with your ideal customers.

Separating Personal and Business Identities

Another major fear I hear often is, "I don't want my personal information exposed." Many business owners worry that by using social media for their store, their private life will suddenly be on display. The truth is, social media platforms allow you to keep your personal and business accounts completely separate. You can create a business profile on Instagram, Facebook, or TikTok without ever linking it to your personal profile in a visible way. Your customers won't see your vacation photos, personal posts, or anything unrelated to your business unless you choose to share them.

If privacy is a big concern, take a few simple steps to ensure your personal information remains protected. Adjust the privacy settings on your personal accounts, use a separate email for your business social media profiles, and be mindful of what you share. I always remind my clients that running a business page is no different from having a professional LinkedIn account. It's about presenting your brand to the world, not exposing your personal life.

Overcoming the Fear of Being "Out There"

For many store owners, the idea of being in the spotlight, whether through sharing personal business stories or appearing on camera, can be terrifying. I completely understand this fear, and it's something I personally have worked hard to get over. It can feel vulnerable to put yourself in front of an audience, even if it's just a small group of followers. But here's the thing – people connect with people. One of the best ways to build trust with customers is by showing the human side of your brand.

That doesn't mean you need to be the face of your business if you're truly uncomfortable with it. There are plenty of ways to create an engaging social media presence without ever stepping in front of the camera. You can showcase your products through high-quality images, use customer testimonials and reviews, share behind-the-scenes content without showing your face, or even hire a brand ambassador to represent your business. However, I've seen time and time again that when business owners step out of their comfort zones even just a little, it can lead to stronger connections with customers and better sales.

If appearing on camera is your biggest fear, start small. Maybe you post a quick Instagram Story with a voiceover instead of showing your face. Or you create a behind-the-scenes video of your workspace with text overlays instead of speaking directly to the camera. Over time, you may find that it becomes easier and even enjoyable. The key is to take gradual steps rather than forcing yourself to do something that feels unnatural. I found that the more I created videos of myself, the easier it got over time – to the point where I actually enjoy making them now.

Shifting Your Mindset: Social Media as a Business Tool

At the end of the day, using social media for your e-commerce business is not about putting yourself on display – it's about building relationships with your customers. If you shift your mindset from "I have to be on social media" to "I get to use social media as a tool to grow my business," it can change the way you approach it. Instead of thinking about social media as a personal activity, treat it like a strategic part of your marketing plan.

If you're still feeling unsure, consider outsourcing or automating parts of your social media efforts. Scheduling tools like Later or Buffer allow you to plan posts in advance so you don't have to be online constantly. Hiring a virtual assistant or social media manager can also take some of the pressure off, allowing you to focus on other aspects of your business while still maintaining an active online presence.

***

Social media can feel intimidating, but it doesn't have to be. Whether your concern is privacy, discomfort with self-promotion, or simply not enjoying social media, there are ways to navigate these fears while still making the most of the opportunities social commerce provides. The key is to find an approach that feels right for you – whether that means keeping your personal and business profiles separate, finding creative ways to engage without showing your face, or reframing your mindset to view social media as a valuable business tool.

If you're willing to take even small steps toward embracing social commerce, you'll likely find that the benefits far outweigh the initial discomfort. Your customers are already on social media – your job is simply to meet them where they are in a way that feels authentic to you and your brand. Next, let's look at how to build a social media strategy for your store.

BUILDING A SOCIAL MEDIA STRATEGY FOR YOUR STORE

One of the first and most important steps in developing a social media strategy for your store is choosing the right platform(s) for your audience. Not every platform will be the best fit for your business, and trying to be active on all of them can be too time-consuming. Instead, you should focus on the platforms where your ideal customers are most active and engaged.

I recommend starting by analyzing your target audience. Who are your customers? What are their interests, behaviors, and shopping habits? If you're selling fashion, beauty products, or home decor, Instagram and Pinterest are great choices because of their visually driven nature. If your products appeal to a younger audience, TikTok is a must due to its rapidly growing user base and emphasis on short-form video content. For brands targeting an older demographic or those that benefit from long-form discussions, Facebook might be the best tool.

Your own data can guide you in making the right choice. Take a look at where your existing customers are coming from. Check Google Analytics or any tracking tools you use to see which social platforms are driving traffic to your website. If you're just starting, look at competitors in your industry – where are they most active, and where are they seeing engagement? These clues will help you decide where to focus your efforts.

Once you have identified your primary platform(s), commit to being consistent. Posting sporadically or only when you have a sale won't build an engaged audience. Regular, high-quality content is key to keeping your store visible and your audience engaged.

Creating a Consistent Brand Voice and Aesthetic

Your social media presence should feel like an extension of your website and brand, not a separate entity. Having a consistent brand voice and aesthetic across platforms helps establish trust and recognition. When a customer sees your post, they should immediately know it's from your store before even checking the handle.

Your brand voice is how you communicate with your audience. Are you playful and casual, or sophisticated and professional? For example, a skincare brand might use an educational and friendly tone, while a toy store might opt for something more playful and fun. Whatever you choose, be sure to keep it consistent across all your social media posts, captions, and interactions.

Equally important is your brand aesthetic – the colors, fonts, imagery, and overall visual style that represent your store. Make sure to use a consistent color palette and style for graphics, product photos, and even filters to maintain a cohesive look. If you're using Instagram, making sure your grid has a visually appealing flow can help make your profile more attractive to new visitors. On Pinterest, high-quality, vertical images with engaging text overlays tend to perform best.

Beyond visuals and voice, consistency in posting is critical. Posting once a week and then disappearing for a month won't help you grow. I recommend creating a content calendar to plan and schedule your posts in advance. This not only ensures regularity but also allows you to align your content with sales, promotions, and trends relevant to your business. In addition, a content calendar allows you to create and schedule posts in advance, making it your social media strategy more time-effective.

Balancing Promotional Content with Engagement-Driven Posts

One mistake I see too many e-commerce store owners make is turning their social media feed into nothing but advertisements. While it's important to showcase your products, constantly pushing products with no context can turn followers off.

Social media is about building relationships, not just making sales. You need to find the right balance between promotional content and engagement-driven posts.

Think of your social media content in three main categories: promotional, educational, and interactive. Promotional content includes product launches, sales, and special offers. While this is important, it should only make up a portion of your posts. Educational content – such as how-to guides, styling tips, or behind-the-scenes looks – adds value and keeps people interested. For example, if you sell skincare products, share tips on how to build a skincare routine or explain the benefits of specific ingredients in your products. This positions you as an expert while naturally keeping your products in the conversation.

Interactive content is what gets your audience talking and engaging with your brand. This can include polls, Q&A sessions, user-generated content, and live videos. Many brands have great success encouraging customers to share photos of their purchases and tagging their store. Not only does this provide authentic social proof, but it also increases your brand's reach to their network of followers. Running occasional contests or giveaways is another fantastic way to boost engagement and attract new customers.

A good rule of thumb is to follow the 80/20 rule – 80% of your content should be engaging, educational, or entertaining, while only 20% should be directly promotional. Make sure to check your analytics regularly to see what's working. See which posts are getting the most interaction and adjust your content accordingly.

***

Building a strong social media strategy isn't about selling. It's about creating a brand that people want to follow, interact with, and eventually buy from. The more effort you put into engaging with your audience, maintaining a consistent brand identity, and choosing the right platforms, the more successful your store will be in the social commerce space. In the next chapter, we'll dive deeper into content creation strategies that will keep your audience coming back for more.

CREATING COMPELLING CONTENT THAT KEEPS YOUR AUDIENCE ENGAGED

One of the most important things I tell e-commerce store owners is that social media isn't just a sales channel – it's a storytelling platform. If your only posts are product images with "Buy Now" captions, you're missing out on what makes social commerce so powerful: connection. The brands that truly succeed on social media are the ones that create compelling, engaging content that resonates with their audience and naturally leads to sales.

Compelling content isn't just about pretty pictures or high-quality videos – it's about telling a story, sparking curiosity, and making people feel something. When you focus on creating content that educates, entertains, or inspires, you build a loyal audience that trusts your brand. And trust leads to conversions.

So, how do you create content that keeps people coming back while also driving sales? Let's break it down.

Understanding Your Audience and Their Needs

Before you create content, you need to understand your audience. What are their interests, pain points, and desires? What kind of content do they already engage with? The best way to figure this out is by listening – pay attention to comments, direct messages, and customer reviews. Conduct polls or Q&A sessions to get direct feedback from your followers.

Once you have a clear understanding of what your audience cares about, you can create content that speaks directly to them. For example, if you sell fitness apparel, your audience likely cares about workouts, nutrition, and motivation. Instead of just posting product shots, you could share quick workout tips, motivational quotes, or testimonials from real customers about how your clothing helps them perform better.

The key is to position your brand as a valuable resource, not just a product seller. When your audience sees you as a go-to source for valuable content, they'll naturally be more inclined to support your business.

Crafting Content That Sells Without Feeling "Salesy"

Many store owners struggle with the idea of

selling on social media because they don't want to come across as too pushy. The good news is, you don't have to. The best sales-driven content doesn't feel like an ad – it feels like a conversation.

One of my favorite approaches is storytelling-based selling. Instead of saying, "Our new moisturizer is available now," share a customer's journey: "Meet Sarah. She struggled with dry skin for years until she found our all-natural moisturizer. Here's how it transformed her routine." This approach makes the product part of a relatable story, rather than just another item for sale.

Another powerful tactic is demonstrating the product in use. If you sell home organization products, don't just post a static image – show a before-and-after video of a messy space transformed. If you sell clothing, create styling guides or "day in the life" videos featuring your products. People need to visualize how your products fit into their lives, and compelling content makes that easy for them.

The Power of Video Content and Storytelling

If there's one type of content I recommend focusing on, it's video. Video content consistently outperforms static images on platforms like Instagram, Facebook, and TikTok. The reason? It's engaging, dynamic, and allows you to show your personality.

Short-form videos, such as TikTok and Instagram Reels, are especially powerful for grabbing attention quickly. You don't need professional equipment – a smartphone and good lighting are enough to create high-quality content. The key is to make your videos feel authentic. Behind-the-scenes clips, product tutorials, customer testimonials, and even "day in the life" videos of your business can help customers connect with your brand on a deeper level.

Live video is another game-changer. Hosting live shopping events, Q&A sessions, or product demos creates real-time engagement and builds trust with your audience. You can use live video to answer common customer questions, introduce new products, and even offer exclusive discounts to viewers – leading to instant sales and increased customer loyalty.

Creating a Content Calendar for Consistency

One of the biggest challenges with social media content is consistency. Posting randomly or only when you have a promotion won't build an engaged audience. Instead, I always recommend creating a content calendar to plan and schedule your posts in advance.

Your content calendar should include a mix of:

- Engagement-driven content (polls, Q&As, user-generated content features)

- Educational content (tips, tutorials, industry insights)
- Behind-the-scenes content (your business journey, process videos)
- Sales-driven content (product launches, limited-time offers, influencer collaborations)

By planning content in advance, you can ensure a good balance between engagement and sales while keeping your brand top-of-mind for your audience.

Leveraging User-Generated Content for Trust and Credibility

One of the easiest ways to create compelling content without doing all the work yourself is by leveraging user-generated content (UGC). When happy customers share photos, videos, or testimonials about your products, that's free marketing – and it's incredibly effective.

Encourage customers to tag your brand in their posts or create a branded hashtag to collect user-generated content. Feature these posts on your social media, website, and even in paid ads. You can even create and share screenshots of reviews customers have left on your website. People trust real customer experiences more than polished marketing messages, so showcasing UGC builds credibility and social proof.

If you're not getting much user-generated content yet, incentivize it. Offer small discounts or giveaways for customers who share their experience with your products. Make sure you're sending automatic product review requests to encourage customer feedback. Over time, this creates a steady stream of authentic content that strengthens your brand's reputation.

Measuring Content Success and Optimizing

Creating great content is only half the battle. You also need to measure its performance and adjust your strategy accordingly. Every social platform provides analytics tools that show you how your posts are performing. Pay attention to metrics like engagement (likes, shares, comments), reach, and conversion rates.

If a certain type of content is getting high engagement, create more of it. If some posts aren't performing well, tweak your messaging, visuals, or format. A/B testing different styles of content can help you understand what resonates best with your audience.

I always recommend reviewing your analytics at least once a month. Identify what's working, refine your strategy, and keep testing new ideas. Social media success isn't about luck – it's about learning, adapting, and consistently delivering value to your audience. We'll delve more into analytics later in this book.

***

Creating compelling content that drives sales is both an art and a science. The brands that succeed in social commerce are the ones that go beyond just selling products – they create stories, educate their audience, and engage in meaningful ways. The more you focus on providing value, building relationships, and showcasing your products naturally, the more effective your content will be.

Next let's look at how to set up your social shops to make buying fast and easy for your social followers.

SETTING UP SOCIAL SHOPS & IN-APP PURCHASING

Social media is not just a place for brand awareness – it's a fully functional sales channel. Instagram and Facebook have streamlined the process of selling directly within their platforms, making it easier than ever for customers to discover, browse, and purchase your products without leaving the app. Setting up your social shop on these platforms is a critical step toward maximizing your e-commerce potential.

I've worked with many store owners who were hesitant to set up a Facebook or Instagram Shop, thinking it was too complicated. The truth is, once you understand the process, it's quite straightforward and worth the effort. If you haven't set up your shop yet, start by ensuring you have a Business Manager account on Facebook. From there, navigate to Commerce Manager, where you'll be guided through the setup process. You can either sync your existing product catalog from your e-commerce website or manually add products. I always recommend using a direct integration if your platform supports it, as this keeps your inventory updated automatically.

Once your shop is set up, the next step is optimizing it. High-quality images and detailed product descriptions make a huge difference in whether someone decides to buy or keep scrolling. Stores that take the time to write engaging descriptions and showcase their products with multiple angles and lifestyle images tend to perform significantly better – not just on social media, but with direct sales on their websites as well. Additionally, enabling checkout directly within Facebook or Instagram (if available in your country) reduces friction in the buying process and increases conversions.

Beyond the setup, the real key to success with Facebook and Instagram Shops is promotion. Simply listing your products won't drive sales – you need to actively engage your audience. Use Instagram Stories to highlight new arrivals, create product demo videos, and go live to answer customer questions. Engaging content brings your shop to life and helps build trust with your audience.

Pinterest's "Shop the Look" Feature

If your store sells visually driven products like fashion, home decor, or crafts, Pinterest can be a goldmine for sales. Pinterest's "Shop the Look" feature allows users to click on specific items within an image and shop directly from the platform. I always recommend Pinterest to e-commerce owners who have highly visual products because it functions more like a search engine than a traditional social platform, meaning people are actively looking for ideas and products to buy.

To set up "Shop the Look" Pins, start by claiming your website and enabling a business account. Once set up, you can create rich pins that display real-time product information, including pricing and availability. I've seen brands drive significant traffic and sales simply by optimizing their pins with the right keywords and high-quality imagery. Unlike other platforms where content quickly disappears, Pinterest pins can drive traffic for months or even years after being posted.

One of my favorite strategies for using Pinterest effectively is creating visually compelling product collections. Instead of posting one-off product images, design boards that showcase how different products work together. For example, if you sell home decor, create boards for different rooms and fill them with products that work together in those spaces. This not only inspires shoppers but also increases the likelihood of multiple-item purchases.

TikTok Shopping: What It Is and How to Use It

TikTok has quickly become one of the most influential platforms in social commerce, and TikTok Shopping can be a game-changer for brands looking to reach a younger, engaged audience. I've seen brands explode in popularity overnight thanks to TikTok's viral nature. If your products have a strong visual or demonstrative appeal, this platform can be incredibly powerful.

TikTok Shopping allows users to purchase products directly within the app, either through shoppable videos, live streams, or a dedicated shop tab on your profile. Setting up TikTok Shopping requires a TikTok Business account and integration with TikTok's Seller Center. If your e-commerce platform integrates with TikTok (such as Shopify), the setup process is straightforward.

What makes TikTok Shopping unique is its emphasis on video content. Unlike Facebook or Instagram, where static images can still generate sales, TikTok thrives on dynamic, engaging video. The key to success here is creating content that feels organic and entertaining rather than overly polished or salesy. I always tell store owners to embrace TikTok trends and challenges – jumping on viral sounds, using humor, and showcasing behind-the-scenes content can significantly boost engagement.

Live shopping events are another powerful feature of TikTok Shopping. Hosting a live stream where you demonstrate products, answer questions, and offer exclusive discounts can drive immediate sales. I've seen brands sell out of products within minutes just by creating an engaging, interactive live shopping experience.

***

Setting up social shops and enabling in-app purchasing is one of the most effective ways to streamline your customer's shopping experience. Whether you're leveraging Instagram and Facebook Shops, Pinterest's "Shop the Look," or TikTok Shopping, the key is to make the buying process as seamless as possible. The easier you make it for customers to purchase your products directly from their favorite social platforms, the more likely they are to convert.

Now that you know how to set up and optimize your social shops, let's delve deeper into using video and live shopping events to drive sales.

USING LIVE SHOPPING AND VIDEO CONTENT

Live shopping is one of the most exciting developments in social commerce, blending entertainment with direct sales. Brands that embrace live shopping events can create real-time engagement, answer customer questions on the spot, and drive instant conversions. It's a dynamic, interactive way to showcase products while building a personal connection with your audience.

Live shopping events work by allowing you to present your products in real-time while viewers watch, ask questions, and even purchase directly through the platform. These events are hosted on social media channels like Facebook, Instagram, TikTok, and YouTube, as well as dedicated platforms like Amazon Live. Unlike traditional e-commerce, where customers have to browse product listings and read descriptions, live shopping brings your products to life with demonstrations, storytelling, and real-time feedback.

One of the biggest advantages of live shopping is the sense of urgency it creates. Limited-time offers, flash sales, and exclusive discounts during the event encourage viewers to act quickly. Store owners that use countdown timers and special promotions during live sessions can successfully boost conversions. The interactive nature of live shopping also builds trust – customers can see the product in action, ask questions, and get instant answers, reducing hesitation and increasing confidence in their purchase.

Creating Engaging Product Demo Videos

Not everyone is ready to go live right away, and that's okay. Pre-recorded product demo videos can be just as effective in driving sales. If you're not already using video to showcase your products, you're missing out on one of the most powerful tools in e-commerce. Video gives customers a clearer, more detailed look at your products, helping them make more informed purchasing decisions.

When creating product demo videos, I always recommend focusing on storytelling rather than just listing features. Think about how your product solves a problem or improves the customer's life. If you sell skincare, show how the product works over time. If you sell home gadgets, demonstrate how they simplify everyday tasks. The goal is to create an emotional connection and make the viewer feel like they need your product.

Another best practice is to keep your videos concise and engaging. Attention spans are short, so capturing interest within the first few seconds is crucial. I've found that adding movement – whether it's showing a product in use, switching angles, or including quick cuts – keeps viewers engaged. Including a clear call to action at the end, such as "Shop now" or "Click the link in our bio," directs viewers toward making a purchase.

User-generated content (UGC) can also be a goldmine for video marketing. Encourage satisfied customers or influencers to create their own product demos and share them on their social media accounts. Not only does this provide social proof, but it also extends your reach beyond your existing audience. We'll talk more about UGC in the next chapter.

Best Practices for Hosting Successful Live Selling Sessions

Once you're ready to go live, planning is key to ensuring a successful event. If you jump into live selling without a strategy, you may end up disappointed by low engagement and sales. To maximize results, preparation is everything.

Start by promoting your live event well in advance. Use Instagram Stories, Facebook posts, email marketing, and even SMS reminders to build anticipation. Creating a teaser video highlighting what viewers can expect – such as product reveals, discounts, or giveaways – helps generate excitement and encourages people to tune in.

When hosting a live session, energy and

authenticity make all the difference. Viewers want to connect with a real person, not a scripted sales pitch. I always recommend speaking in a conversational tone, engaging directly with viewers by addressing their comments, and showing genuine enthusiasm for your products. Live shopping should feel like a friendly, interactive shopping experience rather than a one-sided presentation.

Demonstrating products in action is crucial. Show different use cases, highlight key benefits, and answer common customer questions in real-time. For example, if you're selling clothing, try on different outfits and discuss fit, fabric, and styling options. If you're selling tech gadgets, show them working in real-life scenarios. The more you can make viewers visualize themselves using the product, the better.

Another effective strategy is incorporating social proof into your live session. Mention positive customer reviews, share testimonials, or even invite a satisfied customer or influencer to join the session and talk about their experience. This builds trust and reassures hesitant buyers.

Try to encourage engagement throughout the event. Ask viewers questions, run polls, and incentivize participation with giveaways or exclusive discounts. For example, offering a special discount code only available during the live stream can create a sense of urgency and drive more sales.

Finally, always analyze your results after each live

shopping event. Review your engagement metrics, sales data, and viewer interactions to see what worked and what could be improved. Over time, you'll refine your approach and discover the best strategies for your audience.

***

Live shopping and video content are changing the way customers interact with brands online. Whether you're hosting live shopping events, creating product demo videos, or leveraging user-generated content, the key is to create engaging, informative, and entertaining experiences. The more you connect with your audience in real-time, the more trust and loyalty you'll build, ultimately driving higher sales.

Now that you understand the power of live shopping and video marketing, the next chapter will dive into strategies for maximizing user-generated content and social proof to further boost your e-commerce success.

LEVERAGING USER-GENERATED CONTENT AND SOCIAL PROOF TO BUILD TRUST

One of the biggest challenges for e-commerce brands is building trust with potential customers. People are naturally skeptical of marketing messages, but they trust the opinions of other shoppers. That's why user-generated content (UGC) is one of the most powerful tools in social commerce. When customers see real people using and loving your products, it adds credibility that no amount of traditional advertising can match.

Brands can boost their sales by encouraging customers to share photos, videos, and reviews of their purchases. It's not just about showcasing your products – it's about creating a sense of community around your brand. When someone posts about your product on social media, it acts as a personal recommendation to their followers. This kind of organic word-of-mouth marketing is invaluable because it feels authentic and relatable.

UGC also provides a steady stream of content

for your brand. Instead of constantly creating new photos and videos yourself, you can feature content from real customers. Not only does this save time and money, but it also keeps your marketing fresh and engaging. The more your audience sees people just like them enjoying your products, the more likely they are to make a purchase.

How to Encourage Customers to Create and Share UGC

Getting customers to share content about your brand doesn't happen by accident – it requires a strategy. I always recommend making it as easy and rewarding as possible for customers to participate. One of the simplest ways to do this is by creating a branded hashtag and encouraging customers to use it when they post about your products. This makes it easy for you to find and share their content while also increasing visibility for your brand.

Another effective approach is running contests or giveaways where customers must share a photo or video using your product to enter. I've seen brands experience a surge in engagement just by offering a small incentive like a discount code or a chance to win a free product. People love the opportunity to be featured by brands they admire, so even something as simple as reposting their content on your official account can be a great motivator.

Requesting reviews with photos or videos is another powerful way to generate UGC. After a customer makes a purchase, send a follow-up email thanking them and encouraging them to leave a review with an image. Offering a small discount on their next purchase in exchange for a review can be a great way to incentivize participation without feeling overly pushy.

Leveraging Social Proof to Increase Conversions

Social proof is the psychological phenomenon where people look to others' actions to determine their own. In e-commerce, this means potential customers are more likely to buy a product if they see others doing the same. This is why testimonials, ratings, and influencer endorsements are so effective.

One of the best ways to showcase social proof is by featuring customer reviews prominently on your website and social media pages. I always recommend including real photos or videos along with written testimonials to make them feel more authentic. If possible, display star ratings directly on product pages and even in social media ads. Seeing that others have had a great experience with your brand reduces uncertainty and helps push customers toward making a purchase.

Influencer collaborations also play a major role in social proof. When an influencer talks about your product, their audience sees it as a trusted recommendation rather than a sales pitch. The key here is choosing influencers who genuinely align with your brand values. I always advise working with micro-influencers (5,000–100,000 followers) in addition to larger influencers, as their engagement rates tend to be higher and their followers trust their recommendations more. We'll talk more about influencer marketing in the next chapter.

Another way to leverage social proof is by highlighting customer milestones or user-generated content in your marketing. For example, if you sell skincare products and customers have shared before-and-after photos, showcase those transformations. If thousands of customers have bought a specific product, mentioning that in your ads or product descriptions can make potential buyers feel like they're making a popular and trusted choice.

Best Practices for Showcasing UGC and Social Proof

Once you've gathered UGC and social proof, the way you present it makes all the difference. I've found that the best-performing brands integrate customer content into every part of their marketing strategy rather than treating it as an afterthought.

On social media, regularly feature customer photos and testimonials in your feed and Stories. Instagram Highlights are a great way to keep user-generated content visible for new visitors to your profile. TikTok and Instagram Reels are also excellent platforms for resharing customer videos, product unboxings, or tutorial-style content featuring real users.

Your website should also prominently display UGC and social proof. I always recommend adding a dedicated "Customer Reviews" or "Real Customer Photos" section to product pages. Interactive galleries where users can upload their own images create a sense of community and help new customers feel more confident in their purchases. If you have a high number of positive reviews, consider adding a rotating testimonial slider on your homepage or checkout page to reinforce trust at critical decision-making points.

Email marketing is another great way to incorporate UGC. Instead of relying solely on polished brand images, try including customer photos in your promotional emails. A "Top Picks from Our Customers" email featuring user-generated images can feel more personal and relatable, encouraging others to make a purchase.

Finally, paid advertising can be a great place to integrate UGC. I've seen brands lower their cost-per-click and improve conversion rates simply by using customer testimonials or influencer clips in their ads instead of traditional product shots. Social proof in ads helps break down skepticism, making potential customers more likely to take action.

***

User-generated content and social proof are not just nice-to-haves – they are essential for building trust, engaging your audience, and driving more sales. The key is to actively encourage and showcase authentic content from your customers. By making UGC a core part of your strategy, you'll create a more relatable brand, build stronger relationships with your audience, and ultimately see higher conversion rates.

INFLUENCER MARKETING

Influencer marketing has become one of the most effective ways to build brand awareness, drive engagement, and increase sales. Consumers trust recommendations from people they follow more than traditional advertising, which makes influencers a powerful tool for reaching your ideal audience. I've seen e-commerce brands grow rapidly by collaborating with influencers who align with their brand values and target demographic. However, not all influencers are created equal, and finding the right ones requires a strategic approach.

When looking for influencers to partner with, the first step is defining your ideal customer. Who are they following? What kind of content do they engage with? The goal isn't just to find someone with a large following but rather an influencer whose audience matches your customer base. You can research influencers within your niche by searching relevant hashtags, browsing engagement levels on posts, and using influencer marketing tools like Upfluence, AspireIQ, or Heepsy to streamline the process.

Once you've identified potential influencers, don't just look at their follower count – pay attention to their engagement rate. An influencer with 20,000 highly engaged followers is often more valuable than someone with 500,000 followers but low interaction on their posts. Look at their comment sections: Are people asking questions, tagging friends, and genuinely interested in their content? Engagement is a key indicator of how much trust an influencer has built with their audience, and that trust directly impacts how well your product will resonate.

When reaching out to influencers, be personal and direct. Generic messages don't get nearly as many responses as personalized outreach. Let them know why you're interested in working with them, how your product fits their lifestyle, and what kind of collaboration you have in mind. Some influencers prefer sponsored posts, while others may be open to product gifting in exchange for content. The key is to establish a mutually beneficial relationship that aligns with both of your goals.

Micro vs. Macro Influencers: Which Is Better for Your Brand?

One thing you might be wondering is whether you should work with micro-influencers or macro-influencers. The answer depends on your brand, budget, and marketing objectives.

Micro-influencers typically have between 5,000 and 100,000 followers. While their audience is smaller, they often have a stronger connection with their followers, leading to higher engagement rates. For many store owners, working with micro-influencers is more effective because they tend to be more accessible, affordable, and willing to create authentic content. If you're just starting out or working with a limited budget, partnering with several micro-influencers can be a great way to build awareness without spending a fortune.

Macro-influencers, on the other hand, have hundreds of thousands to millions of followers. Their reach is massive, but engagement can sometimes be lower compared to micro-influencers. Working with macro-influencers can be beneficial if you're looking to scale quickly and gain widespread brand recognition. However, the cost of partnering with them can be significantly higher, often requiring a substantial investment for a single post or campaign.

One strategy that can work exceptionally well is combining both types of influencers. For example, you could collaborate with a macro-influencer for a big brand awareness push while simultaneously working with multiple micro-influencers to create a steady stream of authentic content. This hybrid approach maximizes reach while maintaining a level of trust and engagement with niche audiences.

Structuring Partnerships for Maximum ROI

When structuring influencer partnerships, it's

important to focus on getting a return on your investment. Make sure you clearly define the goals of your campaign before moving forward. Are you looking for increased brand awareness, more social media followers, or direct sales? Having a clear objective will help you measure success and optimize future partnerships.

One of the best ways to structure an influencer collaboration is through affiliate marketing or performance-based partnerships. Instead of paying a flat fee for a post, you can offer influencers a commission for every sale they generate using a unique discount code or tracking link. This approach incentivizes them to create engaging content and actively promote your products. Brands can dramatically increase their ROI by using this method because influencers have a vested interest in driving real results rather than just posting for a one-time payment.

If you prefer a traditional paid partnership, make sure to set clear expectations. Provide influencers with detailed guidelines on messaging, product highlights, and any required call-to-actions. However, give them creative freedom to present the product in a way that resonates with their audience. Influencer marketing works best when content feels authentic rather than overly scripted.

Another powerful strategy is running influencer giveaways. This not only generates buzz around your brand but also helps grow your audience quickly. Partnering with an influencer to give away one of your best-selling products in exchange for followers, comments, or user-generated content can lead to a surge in engagement and long-term customer acquisition.

Tracking performance is crucial for optimizing your influencer marketing strategy. Use tools like UTM links, coupon codes, or Instagram Insights to measure engagement and conversions. If an influencer delivers strong results, consider building a long-term relationship rather than a one-off collaboration. Many brands thrive by turning influencers into long-term brand ambassadors, continuously featuring them in campaigns and leveraging their credibility to boost sales over time.

***

Influencer marketing is one of the most powerful tools available for e-commerce brands, but success depends on choosing the right influencers, structuring partnerships effectively, and continuously analyzing performance. Whether you're working with micro-influencers for targeted engagement or macro-influencers for mass reach, the key is to build authentic relationships that benefit both your brand and the influencer.

Next let's look at other paid marketing opportunities that you can leverage on social media.

RUNNING PAID SOCIAL MEDIA ADS FOR E-COMMERCE

Running paid social media ads is one of the most effective ways to drive targeted traffic to your e-commerce store. Organic reach on social media is becoming increasingly difficult to rely on, and while a strong content strategy is important, paid advertising can accelerate growth and boost sales significantly. I've worked with many store owners who initially hesitated to invest in paid ads, thinking it was too costly or complicated. However, once they learned how to strategically allocate their budget and optimize their campaigns, they saw a dramatic increase in sales and brand visibility.

Targeting Customers on Facebook and Instagram

Facebook and Instagram ads remain the most powerful tools for e-commerce brands due to their advanced targeting capabilities. The key to success here is to start with a well-defined audience. Before launching an ad campaign, I always recommend mapping out who your ideal customer is. What are their interests? What pages do they follow? What problems do they have that your product solves? Facebook's targeting tools allow you to reach potential buyers based on demographics, behaviors, and even past interactions with your website or social media pages.

When it comes to ad creatives, visuals matter. A boring or overly polished ad won't grab attention. I've found that high-converting ads often feel native to the platform – meaning they look and feel like organic posts rather than traditional advertisements. Lifestyle images, short videos, and carousel ads showcasing multiple products tend to perform well. It's essential to test multiple creatives and see what resonates with your audience. Even small tweaks, like changing the call-to-action text or using a different background color, can make a huge difference in conversion rates.

Another critical aspect of Facebook and Instagram ad success is the landing page experience. Sending traffic to a cluttered, slow-loading, or unoptimized product page is a surefire way to waste your ad spend. Make sure your website is mobile-friendly, loads quickly, and has a seamless checkout process. The fewer steps a customer has to take to complete a purchase, the better your conversion rate will be.

How to Create High-

Converting TikTok Ads

TikTok can be a goldmine for e-commerce brands that know how to create engaging, entertaining content. Unlike Facebook and Instagram, where polished images can work well, TikTok thrives on authenticity and creativity.

The best-performing TikTok ads feel like user-created content. If an ad looks too much like a traditional commercial, users will scroll right past it. Using user-generated content, showing real people using your product, or incorporating storytelling into your ad can significantly boost engagement. Ads that start with a hook – something that grabs attention in the first three seconds – tend to perform the best.

One popular strategy is to leverage TikTok's Spark Ads. This allows you to take an organic post that's already performing well and turn it into a paid ad. Since the content has already proven to be engaging, this approach often leads to better results than creating an ad from scratch. Another effective strategy is partnering with TikTok creators to make branded content that feels natural rather than promotional.

Hashtags and sounds also play a big role in TikTok ad success. Using trending sounds or challenge-based ads can help increase visibility and reach more potential buyers. TikTok users love interactive content, so ads that encourage users to engage – such as participating in a challenge or using a branded effect – often get better traction.

Retargeting and Lookalike Audiences

One of the most powerful aspects of paid advertising is the ability to retarget people who have already interacted with your brand. Retargeting allows you to show ads to users who have visited your website, added products to their cart, or engaged with your social media but haven't yet made a purchase. Most visitors won't buy on their first visit – retargeting is the strategy that brings them back.

Setting up a Facebook Pixel or TikTok Pixel on your website is the first step to effective retargeting. This small piece of code tracks user behavior, allowing you to serve ads specifically to people who have shown interest in your products. One of my favorite retargeting strategies is using dynamic product ads, which automatically show users the exact products they viewed or added to their cart. This reminds them of what they were interested in and increases the chances of conversion.

Another powerful tool is Lookalike Audiences. This feature allows you to find new potential customers who share similar characteristics with your existing buyers. I always recommend starting with a Lookalike Audience based on your best customers – those who have already made purchases and engaged with your brand. Since these new audiences are similar to people who have already converted, they tend to perform exceptionally well.

To get the most out of retargeting and Lookalike Audiences, I suggest segmenting your audiences based on behavior. For example, someone who visited your homepage but didn't explore further might need a general brand-awareness ad, while someone who abandoned their cart might respond better to a time-sensitive discount offer. Tailoring your ads based on where a customer is in their buying journey can significantly improve results.

***

Paid social media advertising is one of the fastest ways to grow an e-commerce business, but it requires strategic execution. Whether you're leveraging Facebook and Instagram's detailed targeting, creating engaging TikTok ads, or using retargeting and Lookalike Audiences to refine your strategy, the key is to continuously test, analyze, and optimize. In the next chapter, we'll look at how you can use analytics to measure your social commerce success.

MEASURING SOCIAL COMMERCE SUCCESS

One of the biggest mistakes I see e-commerce store owners make is investing time and money into social commerce without tracking whether their efforts are actually paying off. The beauty of selling through social media is that almost every action is measurable – but knowing what to track and how to interpret the data is key to long-term success.

When measuring the success of your social commerce strategy, there are three primary categories of metrics to focus on: engagement, conversions, and return on investment (ROI). Engagement metrics include likes, comments, shares, and saves. These indicators tell you how well your audience is interacting with your content, which is critical for brand awareness and community-building. If your posts aren't getting engagement, it's a sign that your content isn't resonating, and you may need to adjust your approach.

Conversions, on the other hand, measure actions that directly contribute to sales. This includes metrics like click-through rates (CTR), add-to-cart rates, and completed purchases. If people are engaging with your posts but not converting, it could indicate that your website experience isn't optimized, your product descriptions aren't compelling enough, or your audience targeting needs adjustment.

ROI is the ultimate measure of success – how much revenue you're generating compared to what you're spending. I always encourage store owners to look beyond vanity metrics and focus on actual revenue impact. If you're spending $500 a month on paid ads but only making $200 in sales from those campaigns, something needs to change. On the flip side, if your campaigns are generating a 3x or 5x return on ad spend (ROAS), then you know you're on the right track.

Using Analytics Tools to Refine Your Strategy

To effectively measure and refine your social commerce efforts, you have to utilize analytics tools. Fortunately, every major platform provides built-in analytics that allow you to track your performance. Facebook and Instagram Insights offer detailed reports on engagement, reach, and ad performance, while TikTok Analytics gives you insights into video views, profile visits, and follower growth.

Google Analytics is another great tool, especially when tracking conversions from social media to your website. By setting up UTM tracking links, you can see exactly which posts, ads, or influencers are driving traffic and sales. I always recommend setting up conversion goals in Google Analytics so you can track the entire customer journey – from the moment they click your ad to when they complete a purchase.

For e-commerce store owners running paid social media campaigns, tools like Facebook Ads Manager and TikTok Ads Manager provide deep insights into ad performance. You can see which audience segments are converting, which creatives are performing best, and where you might need to adjust your budget for better results.

Some store owners like using heatmaps with tools like Hotjar to analyze how visitors interact with their site after coming from social media. If users are dropping off at the checkout page, it might indicate an issue with payment options or shipping costs. If they're leaving after the product page, your descriptions or images might need improvement. These insights help you fine-tune your sales funnel and improve conversion rates.

A/B Testing and Continuous Improvement

Success in social commerce isn't about setting up a strategy once and letting it run indefinitely – it's about continuous improvement. This is where A/B testing (also known as split testing) becomes incredibly valuable. A/B testing involves creating two versions of an ad, post, or landing page and comparing their performance to see which one resonates better with your audience.

I've worked with e-commerce brands that have seen dramatic improvements in their ad performance just by making small tweaks, like testing different ad copy, swapping out product images, or changing the call-to-action button. For example, a simple change in an Instagram ad's headline from "Shop Now" to "Limited Stock – Order Today" could lead to a higher conversion rate. Similarly, testing a product demo video against a static image can help you determine what type of content drives more sales.

Beyond A/B testing, regularly reviewing your analytics and making data-driven adjustments should be an ongoing part of your strategy. Social commerce is constantly evolving, and what worked a few months ago might not work today. Brands that thrive stay agile – constantly testing, learning from their data, and refining their approach.

***

Measuring social commerce success is about more than just looking at surface-level metrics – it's about understanding how your efforts are driving real business growth. By focusing on key performance indicators, using analytics tools to track progress, and continuously optimizing through A/B testing, you can ensure your social commerce strategy remains effective and profitable.

Now let's look at what's coming next in social commerce, and how your brand can stay ahead of the competition by being an early adopter.

FUTURE TRENDS IN SOCIAL COMMERCE

Social commerce is evolving at an incredible pace, and staying ahead of the competition requires keeping a pulse on emerging trends. The way consumers interact with brands online is shifting, driven by advancements in technology, changing shopping behaviors, and the increasing role of artificial intelligence (AI) in e-commerce. Brands that adapt quickly to these trends will thrive, while those that resist change will struggle to keep up.

As platforms introduce new features, consumer expectations rise. What worked last year may not be enough to engage shoppers today. Social commerce is no longer just about posting products on Instagram or running Facebook ads – it's about creating immersive, interactive shopping experiences that blend entertainment and convenience. To future-proof your business, it's essential to embrace innovation and be willing to experiment with new tools and strategies.

The Rise of AI and Automation in Social Commerce

One of the most transformative trends in social commerce is the integration of AI and automation. AI-powered chatbots, personalized shopping experiences, and automated customer service tools are making it easier for businesses to scale while maintaining high levels of engagement. I've seen brands leverage AI to provide instant product recommendations, streamline order tracking, and even offer virtual try-ons for clothing and accessories.

Platforms like Instagram and TikTok are increasingly using AI-driven algorithms to connect shoppers with products they're most likely to buy. If your brand isn't optimizing content for these algorithms – by using relevant keywords, engaging visuals, and interactive features – you could be missing out on valuable exposure.

Another major AI-driven trend is predictive analytics. Brands that use data to anticipate customer needs can stay ahead of trends and optimize their inventory accordingly. Instead of reacting to demand, AI allows businesses to forecast which products will be popular and adjust marketing strategies proactively. This level of insight gives forward-thinking brands a competitive edge in a crowded marketplace.

The Growth of Live Shopping and Interactive Video Content

Live shopping has already proven to be a game-changer in social commerce, and its influence will only continue to grow. Platforms like TikTok, Instagram, and Facebook are doubling down on live shopping features, allowing brands to create real-time, interactive experiences for their customers. We've already discussed how live shopping can engage customers and create near instant boosts in sales.

Interactive video content is another trend shaping the future of social commerce. Shoppable videos, where viewers can click to purchase directly within a video, are becoming more popular across platforms. Instead of just watching a product demo, customers can add items to their cart in real time.

As live and interactive shopping become more mainstream, brands that invest in high-quality video production and engaging storytelling will have a major advantage. Those that rely solely on static images and traditional posts may struggle to capture consumer attention in the evolving digital landscape.

The Expansion of Augmented Reality (AR) Shopping

Augmented reality (AR) is becoming an essential tool in e-commerce. From virtual try-ons to 3D product previews, AR enhances the shopping experience by allowing customers to see how products will look in real life before making a purchase. I've seen beauty and fashion brands successfully use AR filters that let customers try on makeup shades or outfits digitally, increasing confidence in their buying decisions.

Platforms like Instagram and Snapchat have already integrated AR shopping experiences, and as the technology becomes more accessible, smaller brands will be able to take advantage of it as well. If your business sells products that benefit from a "try before you buy" approach – such as eyewear, home decor, or beauty products – exploring AR tools can help you stand out from competitors who are still relying on static product images.

The Shift Toward Decentralized and Direct-to-Consumer Models

With increasing concerns over data privacy and third-party platform reliance, more brands are looking to build direct relationships with their customers. While social media will always be a powerful tool for driving traffic and engagement, there's a growing trend to focus on collecting first-party data – such as email and SMS subscribers – to reduce dependency on changing algorithms and ad costs.

This shift means that brands need to prioritize building their owned marketing channels while still leveraging social commerce for discovery. I always recommend using social media to capture leads, whether through exclusive offers, gated content, or interactive quizzes that encourage email sign-ups. Having a direct line to customers via email and SMS allows brands to nurture relationships beyond social platforms and reduce the risks associated with shifting platform policies.

At the same time, we're seeing a rise in decentralized commerce, where brands sell directly through messaging apps like WhatsApp, Telegram, and even blockchain-based marketplaces. Consumers want convenience, and brands that can offer a seamless, one-on-one shopping experience through multiple touchpoints will be better positioned for long-term success.

How to Stay Ahead in Social Commerce

With so many evolving trends, it can feel overwhelming to keep up. But from my experience, brands that embrace change and remain adaptable will always have the upper hand. The key to staying ahead in social commerce is to remain customer-focused and experiment with emerging features before your competitors do.

First, continuously monitor social media updates and new platform features. Whether it's a new ad format, an improved shopping integration, or a fresh engagement tool, being one of the first brands to adopt these changes can give you a competitive advantage. I've seen businesses experience rapid growth just by being early adopters of features like

Instagram Reels or TikTok's in-app shopping.

Second, invest in content that is dynamic and engaging. The days of static product posts being enough are long gone. Brands that prioritize short-form video content, interactive storytelling, and immersive experiences will see higher engagement and better conversion rates. Whether you're leveraging influencers, live shopping, or shoppable videos, focus on creating content that captures attention and encourages action.

Finally, build strong relationships with your customers. Social commerce is ultimately about community, and brands that foster real connections with their audience will thrive. Engage with your customers in meaningful ways – respond to comments, feature user-generated content, and create loyalty programs that reward engagement. The more you make customers feel like they're part of something bigger than just a transaction, the more likely they are to become loyal advocates for your brand.

***

The future of social commerce is filled with exciting possibilities, but success will come to those who are willing to adapt, innovate, and embrace new technologies. From AI-driven personalization to live shopping and AR experiences, the brands that stay ahead of trends and create engaging, seamless shopping journeys will continue to thrive.

Now that you have a deep understanding of

social commerce – from setting up social shops to leveraging influencers and tracking performance – you have the tools to build a sustainable and profitable e-commerce business. The next step is taking action. Implement the strategies you've learned, experiment with new trends, and continuously optimize your approach to stay ahead in the ever-evolving world of online retail.

FINAL THOUGHTS & NEXT STEPS

Throughout this book, we've explored the many ways social commerce can help you grow your e-commerce business. From setting up social shops and leveraging influencer marketing to creating engaging video content and running paid ads, the opportunities to build a thriving brand through social media are endless. But knowledge alone isn't enough – what truly matters is how you apply these strategies to your store.

If there's one thing I've learned from working with e-commerce brands, it's that consistency and adaptability are the keys to success. Social media algorithms change, new features roll out, and consumer behaviors shift. The businesses that win are the ones that stay engaged, test new approaches, and keep refining their strategies based on real data.

If you're feeling overwhelmed by everything we've covered, that's okay! You don't need to master every aspect of social commerce at once. Instead, choose one or two areas to focus on first. Maybe that's setting up a Facebook Shop, running your first Instagram ad, or testing a live shopping event.

Once you start seeing results, you can build on that momentum and expand your efforts.

How to Scale Your Social Commerce Efforts

Once you have a solid foundation in social commerce, the next step is scaling your efforts to drive even greater success. Scaling doesn't just mean spending more on ads or posting more frequently – it means optimizing your strategies to work more efficiently and effectively.

One of the best ways to scale is by doubling down on what's already working. Use your analytics tools to identify which platforms, content types, and campaigns are driving the most sales. Then, allocate more time and resources toward those high-performing areas. If short-form video content is generating engagement, create more of it. If retargeting ads are converting well, increase your budget for those campaigns.

Automation is another powerful tool for scaling. Scheduling tools can help you maintain a consistent posting schedule without manually publishing every post. Chatbots and automated customer service tools can improve engagement without requiring you to be online 24/7. Influencer collaborations and affiliate marketing can also help expand your brand reach without requiring a major time investment from you.

As your business grows, consider outsourcing

tasks that are time-consuming or outside your expertise. Hiring a social media manager, an ad specialist, or even a virtual assistant can free you up to focus on strategy and big-picture growth rather than day-to-day operations. The key to scaling successfully is balancing automation and delegation while maintaining the authenticity and engagement that make social commerce so effective.

When to Seek Expert Guidance

While many aspects of social commerce can be learned and implemented on your own, there may come a point when seeking expert guidance is the smartest move. If you're spending money on ads but not seeing results, struggling with social media algorithms, or unsure how to scale beyond a certain point, working with an expert can save you time and money in the long run.

Hiring a consultant, agency, or coach with experience in social commerce can provide valuable insights tailored to your specific business. They can help fine-tune your strategy, optimize your advertising spend, and introduce advanced techniques that you may not have considered. I've worked with many store owners who hesitated to invest in professional help, only to realize later that expert guidance was the missing piece to unlocking their full potential.

Another option is joining a mastermind group or online community of fellow e-commerce entrepreneurs. Surrounding yourself with people who are also navigating the world of social commerce can provide support, new ideas, and motivation to keep pushing forward. Learning from others' experiences can help you avoid common pitfalls and discover new strategies that work.

Final Words

Social commerce is one of the most powerful tools available to e-commerce businesses today. The ability to engage with customers in real-time, build brand loyalty, and drive direct sales through social platforms has transformed how businesses operate online. While the landscape will continue to evolve, the fundamental principles remain the same – meet your customers where they are, create valuable content, and build authentic relationships that lead to sales.

Now, the next step is up to you. Take what you've learned, start implementing it, and refine your approach based on results. Success in social commerce isn't about perfection – it's about progress. Every post, ad, and interaction moves you one step closer to your goals. Stay consistent, stay adaptable, and most importantly, take action. There's no better time to start than today.

ABOUT THE AUTHOR

Danielle Mead

Danielle Mead is an e-commerce expert with over 25 years of experience working at dotcom startups and as an independent web designer and consultant. She has worked with over 600 clients across industries to launch and optimize online stores that deliver results. Her one-woman company, Duck Soup E-Commerce, primarily works with clients on the BigCommerce platform, empowering online retailers with practical tools and strategies to overcome challenges and succeed in competitive markets. She is passionate about simplifying the complexities of e-commerce and creating clear, actionable plans for success. Learn more about Danielle and her services at her website https://ducksoupecommerce.com.